MY BOOK OF THE DEAD

Ana Castillo

MY BOOK OF THE DEAD

new poems

HIGH ROAD BOOKS | ALBUQUERQUE

High Road Books is an imprint of the University of New Mexico Press

© 2021 by Ana Castillo
All rights reserved. Published 2021
Printed in the United States of America

ISBN 978-0-8263-6319-0 (cloth)
ISBN 978-0-8263-6320-6 (e-book)

Library of Congress Control Number: 2021937812

Founded in 1889, the University of New Mexico sits on the traditional homelands of the Pueblo of Sandia. The original peoples of New Mexico Pueblo, Navajo, and Apache since time immemorial have deep connections to the land and have made significant contributions to the broader community statewide. We honor the land itself and those who remain stewards of this land throughout the generations and also acknowledge our committed relationship to Indigenous peoples. We gratefully recognize our history.

Cover photograph: (top) adapted from photograph by 莎莉 彭 on Unsplash, (middle) adapted from photograph by Artur Kornakov on Unsplash, (bottom) adapted from photograph by Teemu Paananen on Unsplash.
Designed by Felicia Cedillos
Composed in Adobe Caslon Pro 10.25/14.25

In memory of the dead,
and to all the survivors,
including our beloved Mother Earth.
May the gods heed our prayers.

Contents

PART II

PART III

Acknowledgments

Thanks to the following journals in which some of these poems previously appeared:

American Academy of Poets: "A Amazônia está queimando"
Chiricu Journal: Latina/o Literatures, Arts, and Cultures: "Xicanisma Prophecies Post 2012: Putin's Puppet"
Curriculum and Pedagogy: "A Amazônia está queimando"
Fifth Wednesday Journal: "A Storm upon Us" and "Two Men and Me"
Hypertext Review: "A Storm upon Us" and "Homage to Akilah"
Puro Chicanx Writers of the 21st Century: "Xicanisma Prophecies Post 2012: Putin's Puppet" and "Two Men and Me"
Resisting Arrest: "When Snow Turns to Rain and It Is Still Winter"
Weber: The Conemporary West: "Algo de ti (An Ekphrastic Exercise)"

For generously assisting with translation from Spanish to English, I thank Julieta Corpus, Tyehimba Jess, Sylvia E. Mullally, and Sara Solaimani. Also, I thank those who looked at early versions of poems, especially Marcelo Castillo, Randy P. Conner, Electra Gamón Fielding, and Brenda Romero.

At home, I am grateful to Eddie M. Rodríguez, whose constant love, care, and support of all my endeavors see me through each day.

PART I

A Storm upon Us

In memory of John Trudell, written upon the occasion of his crossing over

A storm is coming. It is on the horizon.
It has traveled far, fast, wide, and
taken much in tow,   the storm
infused with lies and nitrogen. Water, air, ground—
infused, our fruit and animals infused,
our minds infused with lies and nitrogen. We're dumb struck,
believe ourselves smart when we are, instead, confused.
The tricksters counted on our being caught unawares.
They knew our selfishness, greed. Most of all, fears.

The storm approaches. (Can you hear it?
Nine hundred and ninety-nine hoof-like vibrations beat against our
   eardrums &
we remain indifferent.) We have our things gathered. Our children
seem fine. We always rebound.

The storm comes and goes, returns. Next time, harder. We don't even
   bother
with shelters. We give it new names, each time, further fire and rain.
We mourn.
We start again. It could have been you or me, we say, dying
in public beneath a baton's blows falling amid the spray of a sniper's
   bullets,
but it wasn't. We go on.
Disaster has happened to someone else.
We venture out and buy more. We take more. We discard. We pillage
   the earth.

The storms take sinister forms, go by *isms*, *neo*, and *post*-hyphen-
   ations. Be afraid, leaders of the faceless enemy, warn. Beware.
Be aware
when you travel we cannot protect you. We will be vigilant of your
   whereabouts.
Our watchful eye will know your life. Long lines to survive much less
   thrive lie
before you. You'll feel shame like in naked dreams but worse because
   we, in fact,
are watching you. We will make sure you don't question.

And when the storm is upon you, when it has destroyed your homes
   and your children are not fine and your dreams of golden roses
   and bright days are nowhere but in the pages of a storybook, we
   will be content in our heavens eating peeled
grapes, sipping fine wines from our vineyards of abundance,
sitting on our thrones,
new gods. We'll smile down upon you,
our creation of ruin,
pick our teeth with your bones.

Tell Me to Live for Something

Tell me to live for something—
to live for you, let's say;
see next spring;
or to do mundane things, again.
Say why it would not be prudent
to leave . . .
this world, I mean.
Let's not be maudlin,
much less trite.
I don't say lightly
this is a hard time.

Tell me, love, new friend,
why you think we, meaning all,
shouldn't find what is in motion,
not an onslaught of indifference?

If all that made countries civil,
societies tolerable, even pleasant,
now and again,
cultures enriching,
a sound, scent, taste of fish or fowl—
touch of tree bark, smell of the ocean,
life's seductions—all gone,
tell me, what then?

Instead, while Libya saw missiles fly
(he said Iraq)
we heard, "No matter.
Let them eat chocolate cake."
One nation or another,

people or other,
massacre,
razing,
explosion,
starvation,
genocide,
police stampede on private citizens
in peaceful demonstrations—
it's what must be done
to keep us all in line.
"The chocolate cake was superb,"
he said.
No matter
who was hungry.
"*Not just any cake*," he added, smiling
for the camera, but
"the best piece of cake you ever tasted."
In the same breath he announced
bombing one country
when it was another.
No matter.
What matters is more for us, he thought,
cake and all the rest.

Tell me, love, my friend, why should I stay?
Cowards go, yet here I am.
(She, who once was my ally, has left.
There's only skin, empty flesh.
She's there, you assure me.)

I had a dream,
walking through a labyrinth of anxieties.
Everyone was dead.
Tell me, love, my friend, from where you sit,
is the view clearer in the far-off distance?

Are there brighter starlit skies?
With no refuge or reprieve,
not a prayer whispered or wailed,
no return to God,
no exit or on-ramp,
I suspect
we've become a
multitude of floating corks
in the Dead Sea.

Hache ¡Presente!

People die
by the minute.
In this case, someone
on your short true-friends list,
a man you laughed and cried with,
called on the phone,
invited to your home.

He went down quick.
But you know
had he a fighting chance,
no matter how small, it's sure
he'd have taken it—
fought the odds all his life—
a black man
from Cuba,
gay
and very smart.
Yeah, he fought in life and won each time.

You hear of his death by the virus and
it all comes back—
meeting in Chicago,
celebrating his first novel,
dancing to a sweat together in New Orleans.
His holding your hand in New Mexico
like a long-lost sister,
reading your new writing and getting "it."
Years passed in silence,
each gone their own way.

Now you take his book off the shelf,
inhale deep the smell of aging pages,
like a gone lover's handkerchief,
hold it near your chest.
When no funerals are permitted
these remembrances serve as testimonial.
Don't be alarmed
if you spy a phantom tonight
moving merengue-smooth in the rain outside the window.
It's your friend come to say good-bye,
Hache ¡Presente!

The Reflection

Once upon a time
I was told not to take up much space.
One day,
I ran in the bathroom with no lock.
Standing on the toilet seat I stared.
My reddened face looked back.
The medicine cabinet mirror
was a fairy tale looking glass, opaque.
Everything in the flat was worn out.
(In a few years the house would come down,
neighborhood ploughed,
families scattered, lives gone,
our stories of arrival, learning English,
bringing our lamb on a rack,
tacos, and sweat to factories and steel mills,
all dismissed.)

In the bathroom,
the obscured child in the mirror,
with disheveled hair and decalcified teeth,
snot running to her upper lip,
was real.
From another room,
the bully mocked, "She's watching
herself cry!"

Fast forward.
I stare in a mirror
in a public restroom.
Someone takes it for fascination.
"What an arrogant chick," the stranger
passing by says,
"checking herself out like that."

Algo de ti (An Ekphrastic Exercise)

Algo de ti
me recuerda a casa;
no la de hoy,
la de otros tiempos—
las tortillas de la abuela
sobre su comal ardiente;
el perfume de la buganvilia
en el jardín.
Tus pestañas estrelladas—
de niñez
como las estrellas mismas
que contemplaba yo, me parece
hace siglos ya.

Algo de ti
me llama en la noche
cuando te estrechas
en tu cama, como te imagino
que lo haces, o en el pleno sol del día.

No eres mujer para esconder.
Los hombres suspiran cuando pasas;
las mujeres te dan un—*Uf. Mírala.*
Eres un parasol blanco con encajes y moños cursis,
mujer de medias rotas en el atardecer. Eres
lo que yo quiero que seas
hasta el momento en que llegas a mi puerta
y yo me convierto en tuya.

Something About You (An Ekphrastic Exercise)

Translation by Sylvia E. Mullally with Ana Castillo

Something about you
reminds me of home;
not of today,
a home of the past—
Abuela's tortillas
on the scorching griddle;
the perfume of the bougainvillea
in the garden.
Your childhood eyelashes—
sprinkled with stars
like the stars
I used to contemplate; it seems now
centuries ago.

Something about you
calls to me in the night
when you stretch out
in your bed, like I imagine
you do, or in broad daylight.

You are not a woman who likes to hide.
Men sigh when you walk by;
women say—Humph. Look at her.

You're a white parasol with lace and kitsch bows,
a woman with torn stockings at sunset. You are
what I want you to be
until the moment you arrive at my door
and I become yours.

What Is Your Writing Process?

With mop in one hand,
cocktail in the other,
at 9:00 a.m. or night,
flies swatted,
roach corpses swept.
Lola Beltrán belts "Mi ranchito"
through house speakers
from room to room.
I hum off key.
Mares fed, dogs let out,
sun beating on the flat roof,
moon rising behind a cloud—
verses take form.

When Snow Turns to Rain and It Is Still Winter

I am a Bedouin woman, burka weighs and drags.
Goats graze lazily along red stone. My gaze afar.
He was a cheerful boy, my son the poet, grew tall like the poplar with
eyes fiery as embers.   My son—

I mutter, as if he just left the room, scent of his soap
lingering. *My son*—I start each conversation as though my heart
were whole as a pomegranate clinging to its branch, alive. My son
writes verses and lives like a monk among hyenas.
He prays, meditates. Say it. My son
locked behind walls. I once climbed the jagged hills of Petra,
hid within its caves. My son sleeps on a piss-stained bunk, once a boy
who had a warm bed, milk, the breast of his mother upon
which to rest his head.
He read books and played with other children.
On the phone now, men are loud and he shouts, Ma.   My son.

Each bead I pray upon at dawn has his name. My lips murmur,
God in your heaven. The chitterling of birds, the desert floor—all the
    same. Why
does the world not long for him as I? God made us strong, this thing
called Mother. The rain and torrents are Mary's tears that cleanse the
    weary.
My son—
soon my eyes will be illuminated with your presence.

Mass Shootings (2016 to 2019 and Counting)

An incomplete list:
R.
I.
P.

2/20/16
Kalamazoo, Michigan
6

2/25/16
Kansas
4

3/7/16–3/8/16
Kansas and Missouri
5

3/9/16
Pennsylvania
6

4/21/16–4/22/16
Ohio
8

5/5/16–5/6/16
Maryland
3

6/12/16
Florida
50

7/11/16
Michigan
3

7/17/16
Louisiana
4

7/30/16
Washington
3

8/28/16
South Carolina
2

9/23/16
Burlington, Washington
5

9/26/16
Charlotte, South Carolina
2 (+3,895 injured; incomplete list)

1/6/17
Florida
5

3//22/17
Wisconsin
5

3/26/17
Ohio
2

4/10/17
San Bernardino, California
3

4/13/17
Fresno, California
4

5/13/17
Ohio
4

5/27/17
Mississippi
8

6/5/17
Orlando, Florida
6

6/6/17
Pennsylvania
4

6/14/17
Virginia
1 (+ 6 injured)

6/14/17
San Francisco, California
4

6/30/17
New York City, New York
2 (+6 injured)

7/1/17
Little Rock, Arkansas
28 injured

8/28/17
Clovis, New Mexico
2

9/10/17
Texas
9

9/24/17
Tennessee
1 (+8 injured)

10/1/17
Las Vegas, Nevada
59 (+422 injured)

11/5/17
Texas
27

11/13/17
California
6

12/31/17
Colorado
2

1/23/18
Kentucky
2

1/28/18
Pennsylvania
5

2/14/18
Florida
17

3/9/18
California
5

4/3/18
California
1 (+4 injured)

4/22/18
Nashville, Tennessee
4

5/18/18
Texas
10

5/20/18–6/4/18
Scottsdale, Arizona
7

6/17/18
New Jersey
1 (+22 injured)

6/28/18
Maryland
5

8/26/18
Florida
3

9/6/18
Ohio
4

9/20/18
Maryland
4

10/3/18
South Carolina
2 (+10 injured)

10/27/18
Pennsylvania
11

11/2/18
Florida
3

11/7/18
California
13

11/11/18
Illinois
1 (+4 injured)

11/19/18
Chicago, Illinois
4

1/23/19
Florida
5

1/26/19
Louisiana
5

1/28/19
Houston, Texas
2 (+4 injured)

2/15/19
Illinois
6

4/27/19
California
1 (+3 injured)

4/30/19
North Carolina
2 (+4 injured)

5/7/19
Colorado
1 (+8 injured)

5/31/19
Virginia
13

7/28/19
California
4

8/3/19
El Paso, Texas
22

8/4/19
Ohio
10

+ Plus *más*—
domestic violence
deaths
at the hands
of someone that loved you,
loved your baby,
mother,
the neighbor upstairs who came running.
Missing also, children and grown-ups
who mishandled loaded weapons,
and hate crimes
that seemed random but were not,
gang killings, drug related
and organized.
Last but not least,
due to psychosis
and suicides.

USA, 2018
40,000 died by guns.

If I Pray

One morning I heard on the radio a boy named Trayvon was shot dead.
Bent over, slipping on shoes, vertigo took hold.

As happened with any child's loss, the earth ceased to rotate,
I said a prayer for all mothers' children, for my own, for myself.

A boy gunned down for his color on a private street where
his father lived, Trayvon belonged to everyone, and we failed him.

Immediately, the scene came to mind—just a kid going out
for treats before watching a game on TV with his dad.

Skittles and a Slurpy in hand, in the predator's firing range,
shot in the back, the boy collapsed, body shaking.

The hunter of dark-skinned humans was declared
by a jury of his peers not guilty, which did not mean innocent.

Elections brought a president who proclaimed
only the good deserved protection.

According to the new president, "the good" was not us.
The president decreed there be more policing of us,

more guns aimed at us.
It was a consequence of keeping the good safe, the new president said.

From Chicago to Palestine our children shot dead on sight.
My eyes to the sky, I pray. Don't judge my mother's heart.

Homage to Akilah

For Akilah Oliver and Oluchi, en memorium

His body was decomposing   her baby   her flesh   child she once held
at her breast. *(He was dead.)*
Death took residence   in her head.
Neglect. Negligence. Hospital sued
over a young man left in an emergency room.

                                                                      Mine,
was incarcerated.
How was it   all became a crap shoot,
fate of offspring   we'd nourished, adored,
gave to our last breath? They—our babies   girls   boys
muchachitos   niños queridos
neighborhood kids—pudgy or puny and picked on
or had too many *tíos,*
Los García or the Walkers   mom had Lupus or *marido* with
bad back & couldn't work.   Nephews   nieces   *mijos*   *mijas*
nietos   *nietas*   sent out to the war on streets.
Society wouldn't let them be,
not last century or the one before   and not in 2018.

A poet   woman   mother   raised a boy
migrant teacher of language   went from campus to campus;
plethora of words in her arsenal   Akilah and me, tokens—
brown   female   evolved spirit
from the Southwest or Southside of any city.
She was a teacher with dreads and a sleepy-eyed smile   believed—
must have—in doing right   doing it strong   for the sake of
showing her son right from wrong.
If you stayed steady, she said to herself (must have)
captain on a ship of two, where Ramen noodles or mac 'n' cheese dinner,
regular night bath, a story read, put the child to bed,
graded papers 'til 2:00 a.m., then started again (must have, like I had)

the child
you raised
would benefit   fly like Obama had. Success—
at his fingertips.
No one would shoot him down in a "good" neighborhood.
No policeman would kill him dead for reaching into a pocket.
No school would hold him back 'til he gave up.
Diabetes and other diseases would be kept at bay.
He'd be ready   your boy   your flesh   your son (& mine)
mi'jo
for the perpetual onslaught.

The time came for round one   bell rung   Oluchi   fists up,
graffiti can,
the newly minted Black man fell.   Just like that.
Just like that.

When she got the call,
rushed to MLK Hospital,
put her ear next to his lips—
bloated and bluish, parched like onion skin,
having kissed their last-kiss lips, swollen and soundless,
felt no breath,
heard no final "Mama, I love you,"   her boy
left to perish on a gurney
                                        her son   her flesh,
she began to die, too.
Slow drip of existence oozed through her pores.
Good-bye, love!
Good-bye, far-reaching star,
a round of green mint tea for the house before we move on.
Joy, as she once knew it, vaporized.

I felt it way 'cross the land   of the free and the brave
(belonging to whites with money and no conscience).   In a world

le monde   un mundo   where no education,
knowledge of couplets, art, or science,
extent of good works,
community service,
lectures attended or charitable donations,
would re-set a heart broken
by a child's ruin.

                                                                    I'll testify
not knowing each other
but by the way soldiers instantly bond.
I heard her wail
like a canine hears a dog whistle, ears up, heart pounding.
We'd shared the vanity of affording good nutrition,
books, clean water, and little league.
Nothing had saved them,
not we—Amazon mothers.
(Somehow, I'll say it, absent
fathers failed them.)

One afternoon, standing in her living room,
tired of beating without his, Akilah's heart stopped.
She hit the rug heavy,
sun filtering through bay windows,
kept her lifeless body warm 'til they found her.

The killing fields are everywhere—
under the viaduct or over the freeway
Chicago   LA   Detroit   Denver
mothers   aunts   li'l sis   *abuelas*
with outlined lips & swaying hips—
single mothers push grocery carts on the sidewalk,
sneak out to dance,
fuck in alleyways, hoping for love again,
stretch meals through the week,

have prepaid phone cards,
spend paychecks in advance—
survive in the cracks.

I'd taught him how
to do shoelaces, his tie, ride a bike,
later, shave and drive a car,
have pride in work, clean house, fry an egg, wash out his drawers,
be respectful of women, neighbors, be an honorable friend.
He was behind bars.
I wrote:
Look at this poet.
Look at her life,
her boy,
who went down at twenty-one.
Don't leave your mother
with only the memory of a son.

Two Men and Me

I left Bukowski again, went back to Bolaño,
both men bad to their women. Me, like the rest,
couldn't get enough. Both smoked and drank
themselves to death. They liked it rough, said
that was how they got their best writing done.

One winter we all ended up in hell, ran
into each other at a café [REVISION: bar,
public bath . . . FILL IN THE BLANK]. Chuck
wanted to fuck. Roberto punched him in the gut.
We quaffed a few whiskies. They knew. I knew.

I wasn't that kinda gal. Instead, we set out to do
a three-way poem. *Tu primero*—said Bolaño.
"What?" Bukowski said. "*No comprendo.*"
"HOW FUCKED UP YOU GOTTA BE YOU CAN'T
UNDERSTAND SPANISH EVEN IN HELL?" Roberto was mad.
"You *illegals!*" the other started racializing the situation.
(No wonder he was in hell. Then, again, we all were.)
"I'M NOT MEXICAN, PINCHE GRINGO,"
Roberto yelled, throwing another swing.
This time he got me in the eye by mistake.
"There are no mistakes in hell," the demon bartender said, handing me
some ice. "That's the beauty of this place."
The guys stopped.
No one had ever seen ice in hell.
Yeah, it was the start of something big.

Othering

Having a light supper of peanut butter and wild berry jam
on water table crackers while watching PBS,
a woman who wrote a book came on.
She talked about married Indian women,
her curiosity about them.

They were private, at first, she said.
It took time to gain trust
and signed consents,
everything on the up and up, you understand.
How bloody "Margaret Mead" of her,
how "Jane Goodall," I thought,
going over to make tea, draw blinds,
bring in the dogs for the night.

After all, I mused, if her subjects—
multilingual, educated, well-traveled—
wished for strangers to know
whether they watched porn,
places where they made love,
how they interacted with in-laws
and reared children,
they'd write their own accounts.

Instead, perhaps sometime
they'd document
the impudent guest
who came to town
for the sole purpose
of blabbing about all that went on
behind closed doors.

Gotas caían en el techo

Tic, tic, tic,

                    tic, tic, tic . . .

Una puñalada
en el pecho del país

y la noche no pestañaba
ése San Valentín.

Un tic, tic, tic caía en el techo
y nadie dormía, ni yo, ni mi amor, ni el perro,

con las noticias del ultimo masacre.
Diecisiete hijos perdieron sus vidas.

Alumnos, poetas, lideres del futuro
fueron diecisiete almas esa vez,

Diecisiete, cuéntalos en sus ataúdes
que nunca llegaron a su madurez.

Diecisiete hijos e hijas. cuenta, si se puede,
las lagrimas de los padres y del pueblo.

El terrorismo domestico con tanta frecuencia
en un lugar que se llama democracia,

ha hecho la muerte banal. Empezó hace siglos atrás.
Hombres con armas, odiosos de la humanidad, amantes del poder.

Ahora, se quitan la máscara, el disfraz,
con la bendición del Señor Presidente. Tic, tic, tic . . .

caían las lagrimas del cielo, y nadie dormía,
ni yo, ni mi amor, ni el perro.

Drops Fell on the Roof

Translation by Tyehimba Jess with Ana Castillo

Tic, tic, tic,
                    tic, tic, tic . . .
A stab
in the chest of the country

and the night didn't blink
that Valentine's Day.

A tic, tic, tic fell on the roof
and no one slept, not my love, not the dog, not me

with the news of the latest massacre.
Seventeen children lost their lives.

Students, poets, leaders of the future,
it was seventeen souls that time.

Seventeen, count them in their coffins,
that will never grow older.

Seventeen sons and daughters. Count, if you can,
the screams of the parents and the people.

Domestic terrorism so rampant
in a place that calls itself democracy,

that has made death banal. It began centuries ago.
Men with weapons, haters of humanity, lovers of power

now, they take off their masks, their costumes,
with the blessing of Mr. President. Tic, tic, tic . . .

drops fell from the sky, and nobody slept,
not my love, not the dog, not me.

Everybody Wanted Everything

Everybody wanted everything from her.
Everybody   wanted
everything   but,
what exactly was   *everything*?
She couldn't give   what she hadn't.

Anyone might get this or
the other. A few—
nothing.   (No one could have it all.)
She'd be wrung,
poured out to the last drop, a worn
threadbare rag. Then, what
                                                      would be left?

No one would get *everything*.

She'd keep a reservoir—
feelings, memories, contemplations,
what might lie ahead—
to push on, pull through, hurdle and endure.
No one would take her
from her.

White Buffalo Calf Woman

Sitting Bull spoke of her return   White Buffalo Calf Woman.
Black, red, white, yellow.
The Great Spirit sent PtesanWi.
She will teach how to pray, said Sitting Bull.
Red, white, yellow, black.   Remember
how to pray.

This was her story:
Two boys spied at the river   the young maiden bathing.
One desired
to take what his was not.
He became a pile of charred bones.   To the other she
spoke: *Tell the people*
North, South, East, West.

                  Remember how to pray.

Sweat lodge,
tee pee, hogan,
hunt,
marriage,
naming,
how to live,
and when to die.
Buffalo White Calf Woman
returned to the heavens, beyond the clouds,
where even birds didn't reach.

Two thousand years ago
Jesus preached on another land, Sitting Bull said.
Here White Buffalo Calf Woman came with the chanupa.
We learned to gather in a sacred circle—

elders with the young, hunters and mothers,
the nearly dead and newly born.
PtesanWi brought them the Word of the Great Spirit.

she said.
Fire, Earth, Water, the Air.

Remember,
The White Buffalo will return.
Restore the Sacred Hoop.
Restore the heart.

Return to the circle, she instructed.
All things begin and end there.

PART II

How to Tell You Are Living under Rising Fascism (A Basic Primer in Progress)

Protests are called riots.
Torture gets a thumbs-up by the president.
First journalists are discredited, then disappeared.
Something similar but under the radar happens
with the elderly,
children of the working poor,
and immigrants (or
anyone "perceived" to be foreign).

Women—
(in their own category)
are valued most for their (blonde) looks.
Others garnish favor if they hold with the party.
The rest are dispensable.

History books are revised.
Current events twisted.
The future does not exist.
(Instead, it is reported before it happens.)
Military parades.
Police are praised for keeping tight reigns.
A pound on the door at night by ICE,
raids in factories and restaurants,
trailer parks and hotel kitchens.
Detentions centers explode
with detainees.
Arts appropriated.
Science denied.
Watch what you say,
what you post.

Where you go—
on foot or
with passport.
Rest assured,
someone is taking note.

Eyes, Heart, and Mind: Take Action

I

The Berlin Wall was coming down.
Dieter and I reflected.
Me, with *india* eyes;
he, with pale blue of Viking descendent,
Marxist scholar, Holocaust witness,
an ally,
Dieter, my friend.
We agreed there and then,
between good and bad,
all had never been fine.

II

I'll believe it when I see it,   people say.
Still, it's hard to take in what you see,
know what you know,
believe what you feel,
when all is never fine.
See also with your heart and mind.

Icebergs slip while waters rise.
Islands disappear, lands dry.
Rhinos, mountain lions, elephants, and birds,
flying insects and lizards that crawl—
creatures of all kinds
are annihilated.
Valleys dry, mountains crumble,
sun collapses,
babies die.
See what your heart knows to be true.
Believe what your eyes tell you.

Soy la muxe juchiteca

Soy la muxe juchiteca—
afuera mujer cien por ciento,
debajo ciertamente hombre total.
Caliento el comal, preparo la masa,
me pinto los labios,
salgo a la plaza.
Te preparo un guiso
de tortuga con hierbas verdes.
Como la muxe—
en la playa, soy señora.
Atrás puerta cerrada, olvídate de eso.
Siempre trompuda y caprichosa.
La edad no quita nada.
Mando yo.
Chambeo yo.
Ahorro yo,
y gasto yo.
Tú me cuidas. Me apapachas.
Me amas con actos y gestos.
Las palabras entre nosotros son escasas.
La fiebre lo dice todo.
Cuando regreso del mercado,
tomamos una siesta en la hamaca.
Somos testigos de la puesta del sol
y acompañantes de las estrellas.
En la madrugada antes de salir a la pesca
me traes un cafecito.
Así, es que la muxe sueña—
no con puro amor
sino con amores puros.

I, Muxe Juchiteca

Translation by Ana Castillo

I'm the Juchiteca muxe—
one hundred percent woman on the outside,
below, all man, guaranteed.
I warm up the comal, prepare *la masa*,
paint my lips,
go out into the plaza.
I prepare a turtle and green herb stew
for you.
Like the muxe—
on the beach, I am a lady.
Behind closed doors . . . forget about it.
Always surly and capricious.
Age doesn't matter.
I'm the boss.
I hustle.
I save
and I spend.
You take care of me. You pamper me.
You love me with actions and gestures.
Words between us are scarce.
Our fervor says it all.
When I return from the market,
we nap on the hammock.
We are witnesses to the close of day
and companions to the stars.
At dawn before you leave to fish
you bring me *un café*.
This is how la muxe dreams—
not with true love
but loves that remain true.

P.S. Bittersweet

How fine to be a woman
lovers don't forget
(however, they may try),
a story kept in a cedar box
under lock and key for life.
How fine, in fact, that
after words were said,
plates thrown,
tears, all dried,
years come and gone,
they'd do it all again, just
to relive the moment you met.

Whitman

I imagine him lying on his back,
gaze to the azure sky, white clouds—unlike
this grey New York on a rain-drenched day.
Notebook at his side, sheets splotched from an ink pen,
pipe in hand, hat off, wispy hair rustling in the wind.
Leaning on an elbow over wet dandelions, he slaps
at a buzzing fly. The poet reaches for language
until evening falls.

                At last he stands,
dusts off trousers, and heads for the pub. After an ale or two,
"Come to me," he'll whisper to a ginger-haired mate,
"when the gaslights grow dim."
That was that—life, then, not fate.
Walking home, pondering the vastness of an indigo sky,
the poet falls in love,
the way old men fall in love, with unspoken desires
and hearts that break into clusters of stars;
with failing gaze, winks back at a bespectacled sight.

Illuminated streets were new.
Everything gleamed with the shine of progress,
railways and motor cars—
democracy in action. The nation belonged to men of ambition,
ladies and their heirs. He, with his rhymeless verses, pertained to no one,
or so he rigorously declared.

On a fair day a friend and he hiked through the woods,
vigorous in thought and perseverance.
They had wine and bread, clever banter. Perhaps
they swam in a river,
and while one read to the other
dried their flesh in the sun.
The poet felt young again on such days,
the feeling a treasure
to store with saved letters.
He'd remain immortal that way,
virile in the minds of romantics.
Rhetorical questions were for lesser minds.

True pleasure came with soup served out of the kettle.
He himself had killed the turkey or duck,
plucked feathers, pulled out liver and gizzards.
Raw heart dropped on his own tongue.
Everything else went into the boiling pot.
Later, he'd call out, "It's done!"
Meat melting off bone, potatoes and carrots
or love—which one?

Tantrum

Right before Christmas
the president shut down government.
Abandoned by military advisors,
he sat in the Oval Office,
colitis acting up.
One burp, two—enough gas to reach heaven.
The whole country stunk, in fact.
Comet,
Prancer
& Blitzen
made a detour to the Kremlin.
Dancer & Vixen hit the pole
to provide entertainment.
In the West Wing Donner Jr.
watched porn
on the Internet.
Rudy the Brown Nose
dropped by with burgers.
In other words, they were waiting out their opponents.

Change was about to happen.
"Get ready," they said.
Promises would be kept:
End Mexican labor,
build a wall to beat all walls,
ban Muslim immigration,
stop China from taking over,
deny the planet was a pressure cooker,
and end all things *Planned Parenthood*.

Above all,
Don't let the lemmings know
they are falling.
Lemmings in coveralls
with addictions,
in white hoods and
equipped with arsenals,
in debt to their eyeballs,
and those with money to invest.
Lemmings of all colors, creeds,
and sexual orientations
believed in him,
not like Santa.
But true, like Jesus.
They did without toys beneath the tree,
without paying mortgages or car loans,
kids' tuitions. Prescriptions went unfilled.
Small sacrifices, they told themselves,
for the greater good, in the name of God
and all Creation.
"We didn't evolve from monkeys,"
they told themselves. "We're 'Americans.'"

Cat's Mad Lick

A cat's mad lick over eyelids, neck   rapid aim
with scratchy tongue, night runs along one's soul, like   it did
when I was young.   This night holds me down,
claws and teeth inside my head.
At the desk,
books read over and again, abound,
anecdotes from life's failures shift to the prefrontal cortex.
My father, for instance,
after death, becomes mythical.
Mothers swim in opaque waters.
Most of all, childhood looms—
a mallet overhead—in full moon
or no moon darkness—

Night gives a deceptive purr.
Come closer, I call,
bring what curses or gifts you bear.
I won't get drunk like Quetzalcoátl,
running scared at dawn.

At last, sunrise comes.
Traces of a cat's mad lick on
pages, walls, a face that never slept.

A Francisco X.

I

Algo presentía
ese raro día.
Esperando,
sin saber qué.
Por la mañana soleada, todo normal.
Al fin, noticia inesperada,
como un viento levantando la falda
o llevándose el sombrero.
El coraje de Ehécatl
o su éxtasis.
Seguido por los truenos
de Tláloc.
Los dioses se llevaban
al poeta de mariposas y paz.

II

Siempre seremos más de aquí que de allá,
decíamos en mejores tiempos,
cuando llevaba mi pelo suelto
y él, una sonrisa de caballero y bigote negro.
Una noche de bohemia le comenté
(mas sin pensar que con ninguna intención)
que su poesía era infantil,
hasta trivial.
Desde ahí, se hizo mi rival,
buscando
mi tropezar.

III

Al oír de la muerte
del poeta de mariposas y paz,
me puse a recordar a tantos ausentes,
los grandes y los mediocres.
La cobija de noche, la pluma incansable,
llamaban los recuerdos—
las parrandas, los vinos y cigarrillos, el mariachi
El Bar La India Bonita,
caminando por la Misión, la Calle 24.
Ya todo un sueño.

IV

Murió el poeta
de mariposas y paz.
Si no lloré,
lloraron sus amigos,
alumnos y
tantos admiradores.
Lloraron otros poetas, grandes y menores.
Lloraron los cuervos y los gorriones,
las nubes impregnadas,
hasta los cerros escurriendo blancas lágrimas.
Coyolxauhqui montada en su trono,
esperando la batalla,
también sacó un pañuelo.
Ahí está el poeta, me dije yo,
asomándome por la ventana.
Zip, zip, zip, iban sus alitas de Huitzilin.

For Francisco X.

Translation by Julieta Corpus with Ana Castillo

I

A sense of foreboding
on that strange day.
Waiting,
not knowing for what.
Sunny morning, all normal.
At last, the unexpected news,
like a gust of wind lifting a skirt.
or blowing away a sombrero.
Ehécatl's fury
or his ecstasy.
Followed by the sound of thunder
from Tláloc.
The gods were carrying off
the poet of butterflies and peace.

II

We will always be more from here than from over there,
We'd said in better times,
when I'd wear my hair down
and he, a gentleman's smile and dark moustache.
One bohemian night, I made the comment
(but without thinking it was with any intention)
that his poetry was childish,
even trivial.
From then on, he became my rival,
on the lookout
for my stumbles.

III

Upon hearing of the death
of the poet of butterflies and peace,
I began to remember the many missing,
the great ones and the mediocre.
Night's blanket, the tireless pen,
invoking memories—
carousing, wine and cigarettes, the mariachi
Bar La India Bonita,
walking along La Misión, 24th Street.
All of it now just a dream.

IV

The poet of butterflies and peace
has died.
If I didn't cry,
his friends did,
students and
so many admirers.
Other poets cried, great and minor.
The crows cried and sparrows,
impregnated clouds,
even hills poured white tears.
Coyolxauhqui sitting on her throne,
waiting for battle,
also pulled out a handkerchief.
There's the poet, I told myself,
peering through the window.
Zip, zip, zip, went his Huitzilin wings.

Fun House of Muted Desires

We got lost in the fun house of muted desires,
embarrassed by distorted mirrors.
Along black corridors
fears sounded like a train approaching fast.
Longing—cellophane wrapped
tight over our heads.
We trembled like trapped mice.
Come to me, come to me—
our pink eyes screamed   pupils dilating
to Coltrane's
A Love Supreme.

When Myra Had Enough

¡Basta!
Her hand flung the chisel knife across the room.
Myra'd had enough.

I can still see her
even after menopause, slender as the blade
that hit a wall and then the floor. ¡*Zas!*
Hair cut asymmetrically with my moustache scissors,
she was the exquisite sum of disparate parts.
Threw things, Myra did, with a pitcher's arm—
chunks of clay, beads, bits of glass.
In her self-righteous wrath,
daily living became prosaic,
              "These are not good times for the artist," she said.
(Had there ever been?)
I lit a cigarette.
"I'm not going to cry," she spoke again.
(I'd never seen her cry.)
My task was to listen. Instead,
"Let me tell you something, Myra,"
I began to yap,
"we'll get through this."
She threw a wet canvas down the hall.
Walls turned psychedelic.
I knew she'd had enough.
"Don't panic, baby.
You sell a painting.
I'll get rid of my truck . . .

By spring we'll blow this town,
the country,
like the Good Ship Lollipop
turned Titanic."
Yeah, that was me talkin' for once.
Myra did a double take
& all I said that day
was precisely what we did.

Click (Simple Present)

I. Marriage

Let me show you *my* New York, he says, over mojitos in a Cuban
    spot on 14th.
I return a week, maybe ten days, later—soon as I can, in any case.
We get in almost everywhere with a senior discount.
Once in a while he throws his vet card down for an added ten percent.
[Viet Nam. Shrapnel in a boy from the Bronx.]

A few months go by and we marry in City Hall, hire a picture taker
hustling newlyweds. [Click. Click. Click.]

At Christmas, under the tree, he finds a photo album with our names
    embossed.
My kids come to visit.
By spring I'm taking chicken soup to the hospital. Central Park, cherry
    trees blossom pink.

II. Le Penseur

Just before we sign the paper that commits us to each other by law,
mail from the Met in his name and another woman's arrive one day.
(A ghost? A secret wife? Pray tell! Who was this who'd left no trace
where I was invited to call home?)
A veritable row ensues.
One night amid fire exchange, *she* calls on the landline.
"I'll put you on speaker," he says, "so my fiancée may hear."
She hangs up. *[Click.]*

A membership card arrives in the mail with my name.
One day we head to the Met.
I lay my eyes for the first time on *The Thinker*,
am studying dutifully when he comes around—

"You just missed Margot Kidder!" he says.
"That can't be," I reply. "Margot Kidder is dead."
"Oh, no, not her," he says. "I meant Jamie Lee Curtis."

III. Modigliani

We learn of the exhibit on an ad in the subway. He's never been
to the Jewish Museum. (Something yet
undiscovered by the native New Yorker.)
At the entrance, bags inspected.
(Are they looking for guns? Someone sneaking in pastrami?)
The steady line heads for the second floor.
A story unfolds.
Modigliani was an Italian Jew,
suffered an unsung master's demise,
died young,
impoverished, undiscovered.
Today, anyone may have instant fame.
But the number of geniuses is the same
any given time.
maybe five.

IV. From Suffragettes to Steinem and Madres de Plaza Mayo

He and I come to live in a world, population two.
(Sometimes it gets crowded. Mostly, we fit.)
We rest, shop, go to the movies, watch Netflix.
Coordinate in unexpected ways, settle in.

To keep things from getting mundane,
there are excursions.
One day we pay a visit
to the City of New York Museum.
both aptly dressed as Haymarket anarchists—
he in snappy newsboy cap, me a Steampunk hat.
It all comes together

in the Struggles of Women Activists exhibit.
We take a picture for our album. His head leans on my shoulder,
dark glasses catch window light. *[Click.]*
Afterward, we won't eat dinner out.
"You must learn to budget," he says. "Anyway, the dog needs walking."
We get on the train, the number 5, head home.

V. The Curator

Two summers in a row we go to the island of his birth,
stay at a five-star hotel.
(On holiday the budget is expanded.)
He slips the plastic card in the lock. On the second click we are
in a room with an ocean view.
("Our room." "Our blue sea and azure sky.")
We share books and piña coladas. We stroll
under moonlight, slow dance on the beach.
The house pianist knows our song.

Our fathers are long dead, mothers too.
Sons, grown. Grandchildren growing fast.
We've done our best by all, we say.
Here, too, there is a museum to see.
He curated his first (and maybe last) art show there, a lifetime ago.
His name appears in a catalog.
Eight days later we fly back to New York.
On the anniversary of our first date
we return to the Cuban spot.
In the Village he buys me vintage sunglasses.
A flood of tourists at Lincoln Center Plaza snap pictures. *[Click, click, click.]*

VI. Masterpiece

A rhythm between us sounds less like trains below ground from above
than muffled voices from the subconscious.

Some days I have tuna salad for lunch,
imagine on such days in New York
Djuna Barnes ate sardines and crackers,
both of us drifting in a sea of dreams,
memories of our youth and the books
we could still make, if only
we weren't so tired,
days hadn't gotten too short,
nights become for sleeping or staying awake
to outside traffic.

The twentieth century needed only a few creative geniuses
prepared to forsake riches,
who might never be renowned or distinguished.
It required even less those
who memorialized geniuses
through photography or letters.
But they were all needed,
these five of each generation, maybe six,
plus four biographers, maybe a dozen.

There is a surplus now, inspiration gone by the wayside.
Brilliant instead is she who persists with no expectations,
is her own muse. She must only rise, wash her face,
give life
another shot,
another day.

When he returns from the dog's morning walk, brews coffee, turns
    on the
local news, I'm still in bed.
Click, click, click

on my laptop,
pad, or pen. *Write it,*
before you forget.
Screenshot. *[Click.]*

Insomnia

La luna no está hecha
de plata,
ni de queso está hecha.
El sol no es de oro,
una pelota de fuego.
Amor no brota.
El corazón es un órgano
del cuerpo mortal.
Te despiertas a las dos
de la mañana
a darte cuenta
que uno sueña a soñar.
La noche es más larga
que cualquier día.
Nada ni nadie
te pueden entregar
sobre las nubes
donde el ojo eterno de Dios
te puede vigilar.
Aquí en la tierra
a lo lejos,
relámpagos y truenos
dan puñalazos al desierto,
los que sufren y los que hacen sufrir,
duermen.
Solo tú andas
sin poder descansar.

Insomnia

Translation by Sara Solaimani

The moon is not made
of silver,
nor of cheese is it made.
The sun is not gold,
a ball of fire.
Love does not bloom.
The heart is an organ
of the mortal body.
You wake at two
in the morning
to find out
that one dreams to dream.
The night is longer
than any day.
Nothing or no one
can take you
above the clouds
where God's eternal eye
may watch over you.
Here on the ground
in the distance,
lightning and thunder
throw punches in the desert,
those who suffer and who bring suffering,
sleep.
You alone,
unable to rest.

Cancer Poem

Feet forward.
Head faces technician.
Clamp comes down   presses hard. They were
lovely, some said,
a pair of violent lotuses rising from a pond.
Luscious.
The premature infant, nurtured on those breasts.

Lay flat, face down, ma'am.
Let the breast hang through the opening.
(Something pushes down, sharp cut. Later,
confirmation.)

I saved my own life, the surgeon said,
having a routine exam. She left most of what now
I no longer show off.
Pain for years to come.
Bone density lost. Memory faded.

Five years pass,
new dull throb,
same breast.
Feet forward.
Head faces technician.
Down comes the clamp.
Take a seat,
wait. We'll call you.
Go home, ma'am.
Don't think what.
Water the crocuses. Make dinner plans.
Take deep breaths, stay cognizant of
how easy they come today.

Mierda

There is a spider that paralyzes its captive in the web
so that it may eat it alive, one bite at a time. We remain
similarly immobilized, our rights sucked out slowly. One
day we may realize we have eyes but no brain, a brain
but no mind, a mind but no body, no arms or legs, no
way to escape.

The thought of such a fate was horrifying.
But I believed that as long as I breathed, hope would remain.
I'd go on as before,
enjoying the warmth
of the sun,
glow of moonlight;
scent of another spring engulfing
senses,
retaining memories of those who loved me,
whom once I loved.
That which sustained my days and nights,
now a fading dream.

Eyes are gone, lips, nose, fingertips—
all devoured. The hour of my death is here or nearly.
The spider watches without feeling the slightest hint
that I could have been of any worth
in any way to anything or anyone but him.
And so, this is how the poem ends,
folding into itself 'til all that is left is the foul shit
that once was what I might have been.

These Times

In these times, you and I share,
amid air you and I breathe,
and opposition we meet,
we take inspiration from day to day thriving.
The sacred conch shell calls us,
drums beat, prayers send up;
aromatic smoke of the pipe is our pledge to the gods.

An all-night fire vigil burns
where we may consume the cactus messenger
of the Huichol and of the Pueblo people of New Mexico.
Red seeds of the Tlaxcalteca,
mushrooms of María Sabina,
tes de mi abuela
from herbs grown in coffee cans on a Chicago back porch,
tears of my mother on an assembly line in Lincolnwood, Illinois,
aid us in calling upon memory,
in these times.

In other days,
when memory was as unshakeable as the African continent
and long as Quetzalcoátl's tail in the underworld,
whipping against demons, drawing blood,
potent as Coatlicue's two-serpent face
and necklace of hearts and hands
(to remind us of our much-required sacrifices
for the sake of the whole).
We did what we could to take memory
like a belt chain around the waist to pull off,
to beat an enemy.

But now, in these times of chaos and unprecedented greed,
when disrupted elements are disregarded,
earth lashes back like the trickster Tezcatlipoca,
without forgiveness if we won't turn around, start again,
say aloud: This was a mistake.
We have done the earth wrong and
we will make our planet a holy place, again.
I can,
with my two hands,
palpitating heart; we can, and we will
turn it around, if only we choose.

In these times, all is not lost, nothing forever gone,
tho' you may rightly think them a disgrace.
Surely hope has not abandoned our souls,
even chance may be on our side.

There are women and men, after all,
young and not so young anymore,
tired but tenacious,
mothers and fathers, teachers and those who heal and do not
know that they are healers,
and those who are learning
for the sole purpose of returning what they know.
Also, among us are many who flounder and fall;
they will be helped up by we who stumble forward.
All of these and others must remember.
We will not be eradicated, degraded, and made irrelevant,
not for a decade or even a day. Not for six thousand years
have we been here, but millions.

Look at me. I am alive and stand before you,
unashamed despite endless provocations
railed against an aging woman.
My breasts, withered from once giving suckle
and, as of late, the hideousness of cancer,
hair gone grey,
and with a womb like a picked fig
left to dry in the sun; so, my worth is gone,
they say.
My value in the workplace, also dwindled,
as, too, the indispensable role of mother.
As grandmother I am not an asset in these times
but am held against all that is new and fresh.
Nevertheless, I stand before you;
dignity is my scepter. I did not make the mess
we accept in this house.
When the party is done,
the last captive hung—fairly or unjustly—
children saved and others lost,
the last of men's wars declared,
trade deals busted and others hardly begun,
tyrants toppled, presidents deposed,
police restrained or given full reign upon the public,
and we don't know where to run
on a day the sun rose and fell
and the moon took its seat in the sky,
I will have remained
the woman
who stayed behind to clean up.

PART III

On the Fiftieth Anniversary of
the Black Panther Party

I

What can we change?

                                        We can

change it all.
Do the hard &

                                        the small,

offer families
safe haven,
provide children
well-lit schools,
books and breakfasts,
care for our aging.
Everyone welcome
to access medicine.
We can &

will
show how it should be done.

We will not—
repeat,   not

be led by fear
when they come.
(& they will   come for us,
traps set with our names
like on candy skulls laid on Mexican altars
(Rest in peace, son. Tomorrow will be our turn.)

We await paradise,
but not without change on Earth.

Change is dangerous   *they*
warn,
a dangerous desire,
most coveted of requirements.

Hunger starts here,   we stated to the press.
we in lowercase,
the collective *US*,
descendants of slaves
from Chicago's South Side to Compton,
up to Harlem, down to Mississippi.
Brown Berets & Young Lords got in on it.
American Indians took Alcatraz,
made a statement,
Pine Ridge.

II

We were young, courageous, and smart.   Too smart
for our own good,   *they* determined.
The Haves charged
with surreptitious advantage,
police had batons and tear gas.
National Guard, fire hoses.
FBI in night raids, guns,
no witnesses.
Nam front lines stocked with us.
Back home bloodshed came swift.
Leaders first.
Infants, mothers, elders
assassinated.
Homes set ablaze.

Second in command
went to jail or turned.
Street soldiers, hooked on substances,

died under unclear circumstances.
Others fell away
on pain killers and insulin;
those no one took seriously
ranted on the street,
remembering when,   wondering what
went wrong.

III

A new century rolled in &
we still can't breathe—
from cop choke holds on the street,
snipers in gated communities,
cell phones mistaken for weapons,
Brown & Black stopped on sight,
one more down without notice.

Turn the page.
2019—
1,099 brought down by police.
White supremacist doctrines mount.
Obama executive orders gone.
Brown children held in detention centers.
(Say it,
Brown.
Say it,
Black. Say it,
Red.) Say it,
Chinese, all Asian.
Bans on South African immigrants,
Muslims, Central Americans, US Mexicans deported.
I heard the Mexican socialist president made a deal
with the devil.

IV

Midnight in New Mexico:
Loud knock on trailers and beat-up rentals.
¿Quién es?

"We'll show our country isn't a receptacle bin,"
the Reality Show Prez announced.
"We'll make changes *so great* you won't believe!
We'll build a wall   to end all Walls.
China never saw such a wall.
They'll see it from Mars—where, by the way,
we're building a Space Force Base.
We have our priorities in place."

V

"From the age of sugar plantations
and aguardiente to heroin,
crack, and meth   in your neighborhoods—
from El Paso to Almaty,
drugs, a plenty,
supply of AK-47s; steady,
sex is always for sale,
kidnapped children a commodity.
From Singapore to Dubai,
Jerusalem to Miami—
in fifty years we've become a surplus,
some joined the opposition,
others the apathetic, indifferent and ignorant.
We are now the investors and the investment.

Xicanisma Prophecies Post 2012: Putin's Puppet

is not Aryan blond (or a golden-hair Thor) but as close
                                        to yellow as it gets,
and orange hued through and through and raccoon-eyed from a
    tanning bed,
a flim-flam man claiming billions no one sees.
                                        He & the Czar
had a chat at the Moscow Ritz,   in a bar,
over *Red Bull*, coke, and complimentary chips,
served up by naked women who took *American Express* and rubles in
    IOUs.

One rat said,
You take the East.   I'll snatch the West.
It's all for the taking for swine like us   and our friends
                                                (ha-ha,
like "we" have friends), rapacious and sly,
unconcerned with who or how many die as we take the planet. Don't
    worry, man.
Forget
        the jaundiced Chinese & as for "Rocketman" (we'll send
    him to the moon).
France can eat escargot. Palestinians must go. We'll suck the earth dry,
                                        You & I,
pillage until we are down to two. We'll compete for the universe.
Fair enough? (Haw, one said. As if we define fair by anyone's terms.)

I, the poet, my head on a pillow or rock, the throb is the same,
my mind replaying Dr. Strangelove scenes,
with no new plots &

no breathtaking aerial shots—
Aston Martin racing along the coast toward the villain's hideout.
No soundtrack.   (Not censured, just silent.)
No scientific facts in this version of a world for the taking.
Only revisionist history.
They are watching, legions in camouflage,
hoods, or riot gear,
ready to take you out.
On your mark.
Get set.

Putin's Puppet doesn't read books,
see films, listen to a symphony (or even the Top Twenty).
He doesn't look at art.
Instead, he shuts beauty down,
the big man on campus with the loyal fraternity.
Putin's Puppet knows one color, said his son—green.

I'll disagree. Putin's Puppet sees color and it revolts him.
Blacks belong in Africa, he opines, and Muslims must stay in the Mid-East.
Mexicans are the scourge.
Like with his father,
his father before him, and so on.   Dark races serve their purpose—
servitude or genocide.
As for women—
you kill a rhino for sport or for its horns.
(A woman is worthwhile only if she enhances
your status.)

How did we get   here? How indeed.
Not without concessions, not without greed.   Down the rabbit hole
the nation went   into wonderless slime.
We are in it deep this time.
I spot the devil pissing in the dark when I can't sleep.
As they say in racialist doublespeak:
I am an Indian woman   off the reservation.
We do have reservations for the original peoples of the land.
Take a moment to think on that.

Detention

I crossed first on foot,
rode atop *la Bestia*.
Rain, wind, cold,
we held on.
My friend lost a leg.
He was ten,
alone.
We swam *el rio*,
nearly drowned,
caught a lift in a *traila*.
There were others.
No air.
No water.
Stink of sweat, urine, and feces
penetrated darkness.
Hands reached for my privates.
Everything we had was stolen.
My sister, raped,
later, raped again.
She was fourteen.
We went on.

Mi hermanito was taken.
We went on.
Our mother was waiting *en el Otro Lado*.
Don't cry, my sister said.
Only babies cry.
One night we were hiding.
A baby started crying, loud, then louder.
Then it stopped.
We went on.

We were caught,
held in la Hielera.
I didn't want to eat.
I ate and got sick.
I slept on the ground.
I was truly afraid for the first time.
I missed my home.
I missed my grandmother's *atole*.
Quetzaltenango was like a moving painting
in my head,
took the place of dreaming.
My people are there.
My father lay in the cemetery.
One day, I'll see them again.

My mother was not found,
the authorities said.
I was put on a plane
to New York.
Placed in a cell.
There is a court date,
they tell me.
A judge will decide
my fate.
I will not understand him or her,
an interpreter will later explain.
I don't have a lawyer.
I might never go back.
Some people would like to take care of me,
gringos and very religious.
Be happy, everyone says.

At least here, you are safe.
You get fed.
One night two kids beat me.
In the day, they denied it.
In the day, everything
is not what it seems.
Outside the window,
between tall buildings,
sky is grey,
even in July.
"You kids need to be grateful,"
a guy who throws toilet paper rolls
at us yelled in passing.
Mi abuela used to say—Necesitar
no es igual a desear.
I desire her voice near my ear,
soft hands kneading *masa*,
aroma of tortillas on the comal.
I desire to hear the bleating of *abuelo's* goats
and the racket of the chickens.
I want the sunlight on my face,
shimmering like the crystals on a chandelier
in the hotel where mamá worked.
She sent pictures.
My mother is in Las Vegas, I tell them.
Is she a prostitute? they ask.
I want to see my big brother again.
He was taken from our bed,
masked men with rifles.
My sister is gone now, too,
the one who was raped.
I want to say good-bye
to someone.

Needing is not the same as desiring.
I desire God's face behind my closed eyelids
as I drag a sliver of glass
across my wrist. Now I
watch blood glisten,
like the crystals of a
chandelier.

Lamento

Los dioses viven sobre las nubes,
encima de los cerros y montes,
pero sobre todo,
en la profundidad de las cuevas,
contaba mi madre
mientras molía el maíz.
Nuestros dioses no estaban muertos.

Si te asomas en una boca de Iztaccíhuatl,
te llama, decía ella. Sabrás luego-luego,
que es ella.
Su voz escurre de miel.
Tienes que entrar.
Se obedece a los dioses,
sin cuestionar.

Te vas caminando en la oscuridad,
dice la gente,
siguiendo la voz de la bella diosa-volcán.
Pero—y aquí mi madre deja su tarea para verme—
nadie sale nunca, dicen.
A los dioses les faltan obsequios;
les falta que no los olvidemos.

El dios de los Blancos también pide sacrificios.
Los Blancos mataron a muchos de nuestra raza en nombre
de su dios.
Nos mataron por no obedecer y por nuestras riquezas.
Matan tambien a gente negra y amarilla. Por supuesto,
se matan entre ellos.
El dios de ellos es muy feroz.

Nunca vayas al monte sola, decía mi madre,
ni por un camino desconocido. Será no por el dios
que trajeron los invasores,
sino por la maldad de un hombre mortal.
Así me decía también mi bisabuela,
y ahora se lo digo a mi nieta.
Es mi deber,
el deber de cada madre y cada padre.
Cuidado, les decimos a los hijos,
hasta el viento te puede engañar.

Lament

Translation by Sara Solaimani with Ana Castillo

The gods live in the clouds,
on tops of hills and mountains,
but above all,
in depths of caves,
my mother'd say
as she ground corn.

If you peek into a mouth of Ixtaccihuátl,
she calls you, Mamá said.
You'll soon learn
what she is.
Her voice oozes honey.
You have to enter.
One must obey the gods
without question.

You go out walking in the dark,
people say, following the voice
of the beautiful volcano goddess, but—
and here my mother stops her work to look at me—
no one ever gets out.
The gods await offerings;
they want us not to forget them.

The god of the white people also demands sacrifices
The whites killed many
in the name of their god.
They murdered us for not obeying
and for our riches.
They killed the bronze,
black, and yellow people. Of course,

they kill each other.
The white god is fierce.
Never go to the mountain alone, my mother'd say,
nor down an unknown path. It will lead you not to the god
the invaders brought
but to the evil of a mortal man.

My great grandmother'd tell me the same,
and now I tell my granddaughter.
It is my duty,
the duty of every mother and every father.
Careful, we warn our children,
even the wind may be deceptive.

By the End of the Twenty-First Century When

By the end of the twenty-first century   when
the last icebergs thawed,
turned warm sea tides high,
a scientist in Siberia
released a wooly mammoth.

By then,
Evangelicals had climbed   an Airbus to heaven
two at a time,
canines and golf clubs in tow,
kids and crosses
headed for Mars, where Jesus
did not greet them.

As pilgrims of fortune
they rolled out Astroturf, grazed cows,
started mass-manufacturing plastic,
planted apple seeds and contradictions,
built mansions with   wraparound porches,
laid out tobacco
and cotton fields,
were innovative in castigating
non-conformists,
(thereby, created a work force).
Everyone spoke ol' English
(while a new patois was born on the street).

Japanese and Saudis that arrived
were promptly chased off
to the other side of the planet,
soon established dynasties.

Stowaway Scientologists
set off a mutiny,
took over government.
Civil war ensued.

On what was left of Earth   life began to flourish.
A new god made of sunlight
or the omnipresence of oxygen
took hold.
Air was thick;
newborns' lungs adapted.
brains and limbs, too, adjusted.
Agriculture struggled.
Draughts spread like a horse blanket
covering Earth.
Tepid waters produced organisms
small like tadpoles,
ferocious as bobcats,
caught for food
elsewise, ate us.
Universal battles were fought over thrones,
queens ordained their offspring.
Interplanetary holidays
called for fireworks
and intermittent peace.

Some Evangelicals returned
to Earth,
still looking for Jesus.
Japanese were back—
to get in on innovations.

Saudis established military training
at *The Settlement* (a.k.a. Mars.)
White Australians went back and forth
on precarious Russian-owned tramways,
hunting for bargains and everyone searching
ways to make ends meet.

Mexicans stayed
(or were left behind),
built a glistening city on swamp
one chiseled stone at a time.
Mayans and Incas also erected
Pacha Mama with terrace irrigation
and three hundred varieties
of root vegetables.
Zulu and Tswana excelled
in imports and exports.
Buddhists reincarnated,
Sanskrit was restored in India,
Muslim matriarchs
established peace worldwide.
Children everywhere were lawmakers.
No one went hungry.

Many scenes like this
fill my mind at 3:00 a.m.
when sleep is the only   possibility
that eludes me.

A Amazônia está queimando

I

We sing and dance in praise of the butterfly—
translucent blue,
gilded wings,
dances—
all its life
from orchid to cacao,
ceiba to banana and fig,
tying invisible strings
that hold our home in the sky.

It must,
lest we drop
into an abyss,
or drift
where the gods won't find us.
This place
where butterflies work
for you and me,
keep rivers full and flowing—
Amapari, Canapantuba and Feliz,
the wide and deep goddess far beyond we call the Sea,
rain—floods and drought,
a mist or fog,
the sun finds us each dawn
after a journey home,
when the moon comes to guide
both the weary and the ready
to pounce and hide—
our home is burning.

II

Menacing fires blaze.
Moneyed whites rid the earth
of the people,
anacondas and spider monkeys,
hawks and toucans,
cicadas and cinnamon,
glass frogs and vines,
palm and rubber trees,
tapirs and manatees.
We hear their screams
and all that dies silently.
A Amazônia está queimando.

They want our abundant lands
and to annihilate our Mother's opulence.
They will end the dance of the butterflies
and then what?
We, too, will die
like in a story told by the ancestors
that we only imagined.
They come for our copper, gold, and ore
Ranchers and loggers raze the land.
At the United Nations Bolsonaro announced,
Don't listen to what you hear on the news. Lies.
Nothing is burning, nothing has been set ablaze.

III

We are Waiapi.
We keep the butterflies happy.
They stay working
to hold the planet in place.
We are the guardians
of our Mother.
Each day before I go to school,

I smear the sweet juice of urucum seeds
on my body and face.
They are protection
from insects and evil spirits.
I sit in a classroom with a thatched roof
and other Waiapi women.
I am the only grandmother there.
I am chief of my people.
I will learn to write and speak
for the butterfly
to those who set fires
and to the ones who may help
save our home.

The Goldfish Went Missing

The goldfish went missing.
Following a cat's tracks
the dog had sent up a tree
before three pit bulls
chased *him* into a field
where a farmer lost two chickens
(same pit bull culprits),
leaving nothing but feathers,
it was a bad day
that got worse.

Clouds passed above,
raining plastic bags—
smothering corn,
chilis, bean crops,
covered rooftops and cars
with impermeable soot.
The whole town stopped.
Everyone thought recycling
went to China.
Instead, it was dumped
in the ocean
and floated back.

Rather than relief
from the heat
we were layered
with unyielding revenge.
Some didn't eat.
No one slept.
Most couldn't breathe.
Moisture incubated larvae,

festered in our intestines.
(Unrelated but contextually relevant:)
Children were taken.
Boys went to military.
Girls and non-binary found in killing fields.
Priests gave penance to confessions,
rabbis roamed through Israel and Europe.
Sikhs, mistaken for Muslim on US streets.

Down with dissidents! commanded the president
through a bullhorn
from the steps of his golf resort.
With weapons in hand—
citizens all for the 2nd Amendment
shot caterpillars in trees.

One day, I took a swim
in a plastic pool.
Lo and behold!
There was the goldfish.
It went 'round and 'round.
What took you so long to find me?
a thought bubble read over its head.
How DID you survive? I was aghast.
There's all kinds of ways to stay alive,
my ally added.
For one, humility to know whom
and when to strike.
Wiser still, know the limits of your skills—
and push them.
Climb a hill with gills,
adapt to flying with fins.

Florinda se fue al cielo

Florinda se fue al cielo,
no con alitas doradas
ni tacones puestos,
pero reposada sobre
un petate de marisoles.
Descalza ha de estar
sobre las nubes,
como le gustaba andar
en la cocina
guisando mole de frutas
o en el solar
podando sus rosales.
¡Ay! ¡Se me ha ido mi Floris!
No te vayas—me pidió.
Aún hui a otra ciudad.
Éramos mujeres buscabando
la libertad.
Ella ahora también se ha escapado
donde nadie la va a encontrar.

Florinda Went to Heaven

Translated by Ana Castillo

Florinda went to heaven,
not with gilded wings
or wearing heels,
but resting on a *petate*
of sunflowers.
Barefoot she must be
above the clouds,
how she liked to go about
stewing fruit *mole*
or in the garden pruning
rosebushes.
Oh! My Floris has left me!
"Don't go," she asked.
Still, I ran away to another city.
We were women searching
to be free.
Now she, too, has escaped
where no one will find her.

Pande . . . monium

We create a square bubble on ten acres,
cactus needles, purple sage flowers,
pinecones spread across
a sand-strewn floor.   Each dawn, we
    inhale air vigorous as the new day,
thank the gods we've remained intact so far.

Rarely is there a visitor (*correction, never*).
Human appearances restricted—
ranch hand,
maintenance guy,
and housekeeper.
They do their jobs,
but not without complaint.
Ailments, varicose veins,
arthritic flares, and high blood pressure.
The season that came hotter than Venus,
no health insurance or retirement funds,
ni papeles. Nada pa' mañana,
just food lines,
trucks in need of repair,
accidents at home and on the street,
violence at home and on the street.
What can he and I do?
We feed the crew,
offer a pair of jeans,
a modest salary,
words of encouragement that pass for friendship
when social interaction has all but been banished.
Alas and alack.
We two are so blessed, we say,

to have shelter, enough to eat, sleep on clean linen.
He and I venture out only on errands.
Communication with family is long distance.
Soon we lose interest in keeping up with acquaintances.
Even conversation at home shrinks.

We'd had our crisis. He survived illness,
a prolonged hospital stay out of town.
Meanwhile, the virus cross-pollinated, morphed,
and adapted to human hosts of all shapes, ages, and size.

After George Floyd
we watched on television
race riots, looting,
and by and large peaceful marches.
We saw sit-ins and tear-gassings.
Not for the first time had we lived through
military occupation on public streets.
Not for the first time did we witness police brutality.
He was born on a US colony.
I came out of mid-twentieth-century Chicago.
Summer of 2020
the gods in their mercy
halted wildfires or hurricanes in the country.
We're so dang blessed, we said, again,
awaiting patiently
the changing of the guard.

Wednesday Night in the Boogie Down Bronx

'Round midnight
six flights below
motorbikes rev at the light.
Windows down, cars blast
from reggaetón to Arab torch song.
Fulminating ambulances outdone
by cop sirens, fire engines,
bus exhaust coughed at the curb;
that sneeze out riders,
shouting like its daytime,
like they got all the cares in the world
and everyone should hear about it.

Bronx nights I lie awake,
ceiling fan does a slow dance
above my head.
Poems I penned
in another city,
season,
life—
pay a ghost visit.
Was that me once
I now see in the dark—
sitting in Dolores Park
with a writing pad,
or apartment off the Mission,
toddler napping,
cow *lengua* slow-cooking on the stove?
Was that me birthing poems
like a litter of pigs
in the City by the Bay,

where in damp summer
a chill settled in my lungs?
Mice whose scurvy-ridden ancestors
came by ship
from Ireland, England, the Mediterranean,
Germany, and far-off China
scurried inside walls where I lived
and beat on a typewriter and first computer.

Those verses had grit—
eyeteeth and tails, too.
Nothing could stop them from travel.
Reagan was grand marshal, then,
with Hollywood veneer,
a smooth-talking septuagenarian,
actor turned politician.
Silicon Valley penetrated the stratosphere.
Sometimes there was café with other poets
in North Beach.
Mostly you stayed home—
assigned It Can't Happen Here
and Brave New World
in your state university courses.

All that set the stage years later,
six flights up on a Wednesday night
with no peace,
still making it on a budget.
What're you bitchin' about?
someone yells up.
(They can hear your thoughts

down below?)
Be thankful you're not homeless!
another yells. Still another bellows:
You got shoes on your feet, right?
A veritable crowd gathers.
Hey you up there, with the light on—
whatchu got to eat?

I slam down the windows, lock the doors.
Forget that, I think, people got no sense.
In a notebook left by the bed
I shape a sentence,
subject and object,
one thought comes after the next.
Phrases look like trees,
words have wings,
thoughts, webbed feet.
I'm writing in hi·er·o·glyph·ics,

a new language even I'll have to decipher.

Keep going, something inside urges.
Nothing's kept you quiet thus far.
Not then, not now, most likely not even from the grave.

My Book of the Dead

For Eddie

I

They say in the Underworld
one wanders through a perennial winter, an Iceland of adversity.
Some end in Hades,
consumed by fires that Christians and Pagans both abhor.

My ancestors too imagined a journey that mirrored Earth.
Nine corridors—
each more dreadful than the one before—

         promised paradise.
You kept your soul but not your skin.

II

When my time came to return to the womb, I wasn't ready.
Anti-depressants, sex, a trip, prize, company of friends,
love under moonlight
or generous consumption of wine—
nothing did the trick to ease my mind.

When the best, which is to say, the worst
rose from swamp,
elected to lead the nation—
I presumed my death was imminent.
Eyes and ears absorbed
from the media what
shouldn't have been.
Had I time traveled back to 1933?
Perhaps I'd only woken to a bad dream,
or died and this was, in fact,
Purgatory—
(Did being dead mean you never died?)

The new president and appointed cabinet soon grabbed royal seats
happy as proverbial rats in cheese.
An era of calamity would follow.
Holy books and history had it written.
The Book of Wisdom, for example,
spoke of the wicked
rollicking down the road,
robbing the infirmed and the old.
They mocked the crippled and dark skinned—
anyone presumed weak or vulnerable.

Election Night—
I was alone but for the dog, moon obscured by nebulous skies;
sixty-odd years of mettle like buoy armbands kept me afloat.
Nothing lasts forever, I'd thought.

Two years passed,
world harnessed by whims of the one per cent.
I managed—
me and the dog,
me and the clouds, contaminated waters, and unbreathable air—
to move, albeit slowly, as if through sludge,
pain in every joint and muscle.
Sad to behold,
equally saddened of heart,
and still we marched.

III

Sun came up and set.

                                        Up and down, again.

My throbbing head turned ball of iron.
Thoughts fought like feral cats.   Nothing made sense.

The trek felt endless,
crossing blood rivers infested with scorpions,

lost in caverns,
squeaking bats echoed, flying past, wings hit my waving hands.

I climbed jutting flint, bled like a perforated pig,
ploughed through snow-driven sierra, half-frozen—lost gravity,
swirled high,
hit ground hard.
Survived, forged on.
Two mountains clashed like charging bulls.
Few of us made it through.

(Ancestors' predictions told how the Sixth Sun would unfold with
    hurricanes, blazes, earthquakes, & the many that catastrophes
    would leave in their wake.)

IV

(Demons yet abound, belching havoc and distress.
Tens of thousands blown by gales of disgrace.)

V

(I hold steadfast.)

VI

ca. 1991

The Berlin Wall was coming down. One afternoon beneath
gleaming skies of Bremen, Dieter was dying (exposure to asbestos
in his youth). "My only lament in dying would be losing memory,"
my friend said. "All whom I knew and all whom I loved will be
gone." Once a Marxist, after cancer—reformed Lutheran. (It was
a guess what Rapture would bring a man with such convictions.)
A boy during the Third Reich, Dieter chose to safekeep recollec-
tions—from the smells of his mother's kitchen to the streets of
Berlin that reeked of rotting flesh as a boy. Men had always killed
men, he concluded, raped women, bayoneted their bellies and torn

out the unborn, stolen children, stomped infants' heads, commit-
ted unspeakable acts for the sake of the win, occupy land,
exact revenge,
glory for the sake
of a day in the sun.

(Do the dead forget us?
I ask with the lengthening of days each spring.
Do they laugh at our naïveté, long
for what they left behind?
Or do they wisely march ahead, unfazed?)

VII

Xibalba (Ximoayan & Mictlán
& Niflheim, where Dieter rightly should have gone)
cleansed human transgressions
with hideous punishments.
You drank piss, swallowed excrement, and walked upside down.
Fire was involved at every turn.
Most torturous of all, you did not see God.
Nine hazards,
nine mortal dangers for the immortal,
nine missed menstruations
while in the womb that had created you—
it took four years to get to heaven after death.

Xibalba is a place of fears,
starvation, disease, and even death after death.
A mother wails (not Antcleia or la Llorona
but a goddess). "Oh, my poor children,"
Coatlicue laments.
Small skulls dance in the air.
Demon lords plot against the heavens.

I wake in Xibalba.
Although sun is bright
and soft desert rain feels soothing,
fiends remain in charge.
They take away food, peace of any kind,
pollute lakes, water in which to bathe or drink,
capture infants, annihilate animals in the wild.
(These incubi and succubi come in your sleep,
leave you dry as a prickly pear
fallen on the ground.)

VIII

There were exceptions to avoid the Nine Hells.
Women who died giving birth to a future warrior
became hummingbirds dancing in sunlight.
Children went directly to the Goddess of Love
who cradled them each night.
Those who drowned or died of disease,
struck by lightning or born for the task,
became rainmakers—
my destiny—written in the stars.
Then, by fluke or fate, I ended underground
before Ehecátl with a bottomless bag of wind
that blew me back to Earth.

IX

Entering the first heaven,
every twenty-eight days
the moon and I met. When I went
to the second, four hundred sister stars were eaten
by our brother, the sun. Immediately he spit them out,
one by one, until the sky was filled
again.

In the third,
sun carried me west.
In the fourth, to rest.
I sat near Venus,
red as a blood orange.
In the fifth, comets soared.
Sixth and seventh heavens were magnificent
shades of blue.
Days and nights without end became
variations of black.
Most wondrously,
God dwelled there,
a god of two heads,
female and male,
pulled out arrows
that pierced skin on my trek.
"Rainmakers belong to us," the dual god spoke,
his-her hand as gentle as his-her voice was harsh.
Realizing I was alive I trembled.
"You have much to do," he-she directed.
Long before on Earth a Tlaxcaltec healer
of great renown crowned me
granicera,
placed bolts of lightning in my pouch.
I walked the red road.

Then came the venom
and the rise of demons
like jaguars devouring human hearts.
They brought drought,
tornados, earthquakes, and hurricanes—
every kind of loss and pain.
The chaos caused confusion,
ignorance became a blight.
(Instead of left, I'd turned right,

believed it day when it was night.
I voyaged south or maybe north through infinity,
wept obsidian tears before the dual god—
"Send me back, please," I cried.
"My dear ones mourn me.")

X

The Plumed Serpent's conch blew,
a swarm of bees flew out from the shell.
Angels broke giant pots that sounded like thunder.
Gods caused all manner of distraction
so that I might descend without danger.
Hastily, I tred along cliffs, mountain paths,
past goat herds and languishing cows.
A small dog kept up as we followed
the magenta ribbons of dawn.
I rode a mule at one point,
glided like a feather in air at another,
ever drifting toward
my son,
the granddaughter of copper hair,
sound of a pounding drum—
we found you there, my love,
waiting by the shore,
our return.

Notes

"Gotas caían en el techo / Drops Fell on the Roof": On February 14, 2018, Nikolas Jacob Cruz opened fire with a semiautomatic rifle at Marjory Stoneman Douglas High School in Parkland, Florida, killing seventeen people and injuring seventeen others.

"Tantrum": The third partial shutdown of the United States government of 2018–2019 began December 22, 2018, due to the United States Congress and the president's inability to agree on the timely appropriation of sufficient funds for the 2019 fiscal year. It resulted from a demand by the President for $5.7 billion in federal funds to build a new US–Mexico border wall, and the refusal by Congress to agree to his funding demand. The shutdown lasted thirty-five days and cost the country an estimated 11 billion dollars.

"(Xicanisma Prophecies Post 2012): Putin's Puppet": I coined the term Xicanisma in the 1980s as Chicana activists and scholars began to form our own feminism. It is discussed at length in my book *Massacre of the Dreamers: Essays on Xicanisma* (Albuquerque: UNM Press, 2014).

"A Amazônia está queimando": I refer here to the current president of Brazil, Jair Bolsonaro.

"My Book of the Dead": The Ancestors' predictions referred to in this poem are the Mayan apocalypse predictions of 2012.